DECADES

T·H·E EIGHTIES

Edward Grey

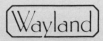

DECADES

The Fifties
The Sixties
The Seventies
The Eighties

First published in 1989 by
Wayland (Publishers) Ltd
61 Western Road, Hove
East Sussex BN3 1JD, England

Edited by Roger Coote
Designed by Helen White·
Series Consultant: Stuart Laing
Dean of Cultural and Community Studies
University of Sussex

British Library Cataloguing in Publication Data

Grey, Edward
The eighties. – (Decades)
1. Great Britain. Social life.
I. Title II. Coote, Roger III. Series
941.085'8

ISBN 1 85210 725 1

Typeset by Direct Image Photosetting Ltd
Hove, East Sussex, England
Printed in Italy by G. Canale and C.S.p.A., Turin
Bound in Belgium by Casterman S.A.

Contents

Introduction

In times of hardship people often turn to established customs and values for reassurance. In a sense, that was what happened in the 1980s. The decade began amid a business slump and widespread unemployment. These brought conservative politicians to the fore: in the United States Ronald Reagan was president from 1981–89 and in Britain Margaret Thatcher was prime minister throughout the whole decade. They shared similar ideas. Both stressed the importance of hard work, individual effort and family values in a nation's life. They tended to be scornful of people who expected the state to solve their problems for them. And they placed great emphasis on national pride.

Permissiveness, the idea that young people should be free to do as they please, had started to go out of fashion in the seventies. During the eighties this trend accelerated. In the United States there was a return to traditional religious faith through the

Above Soviet premier Mikhail Gorbachev and US President Ronald Reagan embrace after concluding a historic arms agreement in 1987.

Born Again Christian movement. And throughout the world the alarming new disease of Aids made people more cautious of casual sex.

All of this meant that teenagers could not afford to be as rebellious as earlier generations had been. Those who found a job or whose parents were in work might expect a comfortable life, with many exciting new gadgets available, such as videos, computer games, personal stereos and CD players. Some teenagers facing un-employment, however, experienced real despair. Heroin addiction and glue-sniffing created serious problems, particularly among the young unemployed.

The threat of nuclear war also created concern. For much of the decade there was great rivalry between the United States and the Soviet Union. Tensions were so great that the Americans refused to attend the 1980 Olympic Games in Moscow, and the Russians refused to attend the Games held four years later in Los Angeles. In 1985, however, Mikhail Gorbachev came to power in the Soviet Union. His policies brought a greater degree of democracy and openness to his country, and helped to ease tensions with the United States. In 1987, the two superpowers signed an important nuclear arms agreement.

Teenagers did campaign widely for nuclear disarmament. But they did not quite have the prominence in society that earlier generations had enjoyed. It is often said that teenage culture fragmented, or broke up, in the eighties. No single movement caught people's imagination in the way that the hippies had done in the sixties or the punks in the seventies. Instead there was a host of small cultures. They ranged from the very smart, conservative youngsters known as 'preppies' to fans of the tough rap music which came out of the black ghettoes in the United States. The various groups had little in common with one another.

Youth culture did not die out, however — it had simply become much more varied. World-wide music and fashion industries catered to the wealth of different tastes and there were many positive signs for the future. One of these was the rise of global rock concerts, held to raise money for charity. At the famous Live Aid event of 1985 pop stars from all over the world came together for a concert which raised £50 million for famine relief in Africa. It was watched by 1,500 million people in 160 countries, all linked by satellite communications. Youth culture was taking on large responsibilities, and helping to bind people together world-wide.

Below A Japanese poster warns against Aids. The disease cannot be transmitted simply by kissing, but it did make teenagers more cautious about sex.

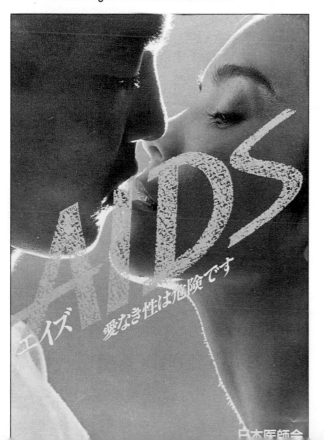

Fashion

During the seventies punks had created a harsh sort of anti-style by wearing ripped clothes, zip fasteners and safety pins. But in the early eighties a handful of young trendsetters brought back a taste for glamour and fantasy in clothing. They were nick-named the New Romantics and they took delight in dressing up; whether as pirates, highwaymen, matadors or gypsies. Frilly shirts, satin knickerbockers and sashes were all part of the look which had some influence on high street fashions in the early part of the decade.

Above 'New Romantics' photographed in the King's Road, Chelsea, which had long been a centre for youth fashions in Britain.

There were many revivals of past styles, too, such as fifties mens' suits and the sixties miniskirt. Punk styles themselves never died out entirely but they had lost the raw power to shock. Mohican haircuts, dyed in bright colours, had become a fantastically ornamental fashion device.

Classic style

Probably the most surprising teenage trend, however, was the return to the cool, traditional look of expensive adult clothing. People first noticed what was happening in the United States where the 'preppy look' spread in 1980−81. For years fashionable youngsters had been using bizarre styles to stand out from the adult world. Now, they seemed to want to join in, copying the traditional styles which rich young preparatory students (or 'preppies') had been wearing for years. Clothing included blue blazers, Shetland sweaters and white-soled boating shoes known as 'top-siders'. Expensive Lacoste shirts with the distinctive alligator badge were also typical.

The *Official Preppy Handbook*, a humorous look at the style, became a bestseller and the trend inspired a similar craze in Britain. People started to copy the type of clothing worn by so-called Sloane Rangers, public school types who owed their nickname to the residential area around Sloane Square in London. The Barbour, a weatherproof waxed jacket worn by 'Sloanes' in the country, became a very fashionable item. And fascination with upper-class style was increased through the press attention given to Prince Charles's young fiancé, Lady Diana Spencer. The couple married in 1981, and 'Princess Di' became a fashion symbol for many young women world-wide.

Designer labels

With this smart trend came a craze for 'designer labels' on clothing. Anything which bore the imprint of an expensive fashion

Below Classic style returns to male clothing. This American model displays the smooth, sophisticated look favoured by many young men in the eighties. The jacket is tailored at the waist and has slightly padded shoulders.

Below A youth models Levi 501s. The look recalls the fifties, but the mass of jacket badges was a fashion of the eighties.

house became desirable, partly because it suggested a rich and privileged lifestyle. American designers, such as Calvin Klein and Ralph Lauren, created especially cool, relaxed clothes based on traditional jackets, trousers, skirts and shirts. Farrah, Pringle and Fiorucci were three other famous labels to be seen wearing.

Throughout the eighties people showed a passion for health and fitness, and many items of sportswear, such as tracksuits, cycling shorts and trainers, became fashionable as casual wear. They were created for slim, lean bodies and the labels again had a lot of importance. Many teenagers felt that their trainers *had* to be by Nike, Reebok or Adidas.

Cheap denim jeans had long been standard wear for teenagers around the world but they went out of fashion in the early eighties. If jeans were worn at all they had to have a designer label – or be authentic Levi 501s.

Flat tops and designer stubble

Male teenagers tended to wear their hair short and neat in the eighties. One of the most distinctive styles of the time was the 'flat top' or wedge, which looked very much as the names suggest. The hair was shaved very close at the sides and stood up in a perfectly straight wedge of bristles on top. In some ways it recalled the crew cuts of American servicemen, but the most extreme examples were so geometrical that they gave people's heads a futuristic, robot look. Designers of the time were fascinated with advanced technology; the flat top was a sort of 'hi-tech' hair-style.

Older teenagers liked to visit nightclubs and cocktail bars where jazz underwent a big revival. For the smooth, sophisticated look,

Above Typically cool, relaxed clothes designed by Ralph Lauren. The masculine style of the woman's clothes reflects changing attitudes to women in society.

Above A flat-top haircut, worn here with a white turtleneck. Notice the ear-ring, an accessory often adopted by male teenagers in the late eighties.

young men might wear a black turtleneck sweater, and black remained a fashionable colour for both sexes throughout much of the decade.

As with all trends, the smooth look began to lose its appeal as time passed, and young men started to cultivate a rougher appearance. One fad was for stylish young men to go about unshaven — it was said that they had 'designer stubble'. Designer jeans were sold with shredded tears in them, and the style even reached high street shops.

Female style

Teenage girls also reacted against too sophisticated a style. In the mid-eighties, for example, pop star Madonna created a deliberately trashy look which included sexy black lingerie worn with beads, crucifixes and make-up, and it quickly caught on with teenage girls. Some feminists objected to the style, believing that it showed a return to old-fashioned ways of looking at women merely as playthings for men. However, others saw

it as an expression of young women's new confidence in themselves; girls could wear what they pleased without feeling embarrassed or threatened.

In general, clothing styles for older, working women had become increasingly masculine as they took more part in society. No one was surprised to see women in trousers. So it became possible to play around for pure fun with more feminine ideas. Variety was the theme of the eighties. Every teenage girl was free to put together her own look according to her taste or mood. And some very mixed styles emerged. For example, girls might wear a short, flouncy skirt — but with men's clumpy shoes. The footwear was a comment on the skirt, and showed that the girl was in control of her own image.

Below Beads, bangles and black lace contributed to the look of pop star Madonna, who had a string of hit singles in the eighties.

Pop Music

In July 1985 some of the world's best-known pop stars took part in a marathon concert to raise money for famine victims in Africa. Some performed at Wembley Stadium in London; others at the JFK Stadium in Philadelphia. The 16-hour event was beamed around the world by satellite television and, apart from the huge sums of money raised, it showed the enormous importance which pop music now played in people's lives. It had become a global form of entertainment, not only for teenagers but for whole families.

Above Annie Lennox and Dave Stewart of the Eurythmics had more top ten hits than any other male/female duo in pop history.

Many other concerts were held to aid worthwhile causes, and records were issued to raise money for charity. Pop stars had come to realize that their lives were significant to millions of people. Their influence could be used to try and change the world for the better.

New sounds

By the eighties, technology had brought a new generation of electronic instruments, such as synthesizers, drum machines and computerized keyboards. They created a very clean, clear sound, sometimes known as 'electro-pop', which fitted in with the hi-tech design ideas of the eighties. Groups such as Ultravox, Human League, Depeche Mode and the Eurythmics were among the first to exploit the synthesizer sound and they produced many successful singles and albums. Synthesizers had other possibilities, too. In 1986, French composer Jean-Michel Jarre attracted a world-record audience of 1.3 million people for a concert at Houston in Texas, which combined electronic music with laser light shows.

Developments like these meant that old-fashioned drum-and-guitar groups, playing to live audiences, went out of style for a while. The pulsing, synthetic beat was particularly well suited to disco music, and synthesizer groups such as the Pet Shop Boys rarely played live, preferring to concentrate on perfecting their sound in the studio.

New electronic equipment was also used to create extraordinary mixtures of sound that might combine taped voices, electronic drum beats and snatches of music from other records. So long as it was all held together by a steady dance rhythm the possibilities were endless. *Pump Up the Volume*, a smash hit for MARRS in 1987, was an example of what was loosely termed House Music.

Another craze was for hip hop or rap. This was a form of music which grew up in the black ghettoes of the United States and involved talking in rhyme against a musical background. The style developed in discos and dance clubs, where the performer was usually a disc jockey (DJ). The DJ or a partner might 'scratch' a record rhythmically in time to the music. The sounds could be very harsh, and some rap artists such as Public Enemy deliberately cultivated a cold, aggressive image. The Beastie Boys, a white teenage rap group, made headlines throughout the world by shocking audiences and the press with their behaviour both on and off stage.

Below Rap group Public Enemy pose in berets, dark glasses and military-style clothing. Their outfits recall the uniform of the revolutionary Black Panther movement of the sixties. 'Hard Rap' artists like these often expressed anger and hostility, in the rebellious tradition of pop music.

Gender in rock

Towards the end of the eighties female rap artists, such as Salt 'N' Pepa, began to emerge. In fact, throughout the eighties, women were very prominent in the charts. Solo artists included Madonna, Whitney Houston, Tracy Chapman and Suzanne Vega. Female groups such as the Bangles were no longer treated as great curiosities, and women were seen much more as drummers, sax players or guitarists in mixed-sex groups. Some very young teenage singers had chart hits too, including Debbie Gibson and Tiffany.

Artists might also play around with their gender roles. Annie Lennox of the Eurythmics, for example, sometimes appeared in a man's suit with close cropped hair which gave her a very masculine look. At other times she might emphasize her femininity by wearing a long wig and lipstick. Pop star Boy George of Culture Club played around with the same idea. In his early appearances he wore girls' skirts with his hair in long plaits and ribbons. 'I'm just a show off,' he explained.

In the United States both Annie Lennox and Boy George had their TV appearances limited by cable TV executives who feared that viewers might find them offensive. But the stars' aim was not really to shock audiences. They wanted to question traditional ideas of what a man and woman ought to look like, and explore the variety of possibilities. Gay groups such as the Communards also won chart success, members making no secret of their homosexuality.

The musical mix

Variety was the theme of eighties music as it was of eighties fashion. Just as male

Facing page Boy George, controversial lead singer of the pop group Culture Club. They shot to the top of the charts with the single *Do You Really Want to Hurt Me?* in 1982.

Below Salt 'N' Pepa photographed in 1988. They were two of the new female rap artists who emerged towards the end of the eighties, transforming what had been a very masculine musical form.

and female performers were seen more and more playing alongside one another, so mixed-race groups became more common. Britain's UB40 was one example, playing pop reggae. The big charity rock concerts gave many artists from the developing world their first chance to play before large Western audiences, and some musicians were keen to experiment with as many influences as possible. World music included Yemenite songs and Bulgarian folk music, the Latin Salsa beat and the sounds of the black townships of South Africa.

There were many nostalgic revivals too. The American superstar Prince was just one of many artists who played around with images of sixties psychedelia. And heavy rock music made a big comeback with groups such as Bon Jovi, Def Leppard and

Above Michael Jackson on stage in 1988. He had been a child star in the early seventies and went on to become the most successful artist of the eighties.

Above Bruce Springsteen performs at Wembley Stadium in 1985, the year when his *I'm on Fire/Born in the USA* single was a hit world-wide. Notice the singer's face, projected on to the giant video screen.

Australia's INXS. They appealed to many teenagers who preferred the noise and drama of big stadium concerts to a synthetic disco beat. Bruce Springsteen had massive success by drawing on images from the lives of ordinary American working men. And Ireland's U2 also promoted live music, creating a unique rock sound with a spiritual and visionary quality.

Superstars and indie groups

The most successful figure of the eighties was Michael Jackson. He had been a child star in the seventies and went on to create a solo career built around his remarkable singing and dancing talent. His *Thriller* album sold more than 35 million copies in the eighties, making it by far the best-selling album of all time. It was rumoured that the superstar visited a plastic surgeon and that he used a life-prolonging oxygen tent. Such rumours only contributed to his fame.

Pop music was now a very big business, and such large sums of money were spent on launching groups that the record companies became nervous of making mistakes. Occasional hit singles were not enough; the companies wanted artists who could be relied on to sell albums over several years.

One result was the rise of small independent record companies known as 'indies'. They were less worried about reaching mass audiences and more keen to experiment with new, unusual acts. Probably the most respected of the indie groups was the Smiths, whose lead singer, Steven Morrissey, sang mournful songs with awkward, honest lyrics about the life of a shy teenager in rainy Manchester in the north of England. The Smiths developed an enormous cult following both in Britain and in the United States.

Above Morrissey, lead singer with The Smiths. The group made its reputation with songs that included *Heaven Knows I'm Miserable Now* (1984).

The Media

Teenage magazines helped to spread new music and fashion ideas. But the general trend was against too much serious thinking about youth culture. People wanted sheer fun. In the United States bestsellers included *Seventeen, Mademoiselle* and *Teen*; in Britain, the colourful, jokey *Smash Hits* became a huge success while other popular magazines were *Mizz* and *Just Seventeen*.

Above A punk of the eighties watching a pop video.

CDs and personal stereos

Audio equipment became much more sophisticated in the eighties. In 1982 the Japanese firm of Sony launched the first compact disc (CD) players. These used laser technology to produce recorded sound of much higher quality than earlier tapes and records. CD players were expensive, but they found their way into many homes nonetheless, and they became a kind of status symbol; that is, they showed the owners to be people who had achieved a certain level of wealth.

Personal stereos, however, had a much more direct impact on teenage life. The first, the Sony Walkman, was introduced in 1978 and during the eighties cheap copies were produced at prices that ordinary youngsters could afford. The stereo headphones probably contributed to the variety of different musical styles that flourished in the eighties. In the days when teenagers had listened chiefly to transistor radios they tended to pick up new tastes together. But with stereo headsets, young people pursued more private interests.

Personal stereos suited the fitness craze of the eighties, since they could be worn when jogging, for example. And they also contributed to the increasing sales of cassettes: during the eighties cassettes outsold record albums.

Cable and video

Cable TV also appeared in the eighties. This is a system by which TV programmes are delivered to subscribers' homes by cable instead of being broadcast through the airwaves. The system proved a big success in the United States, where separate channels were set up for non-stop films, music videos, news, sports and so on. By 1985 almost half of all US homes were linked to the system, and MTV (the music television channel) was particularly popular with teenage viewers.

In Britain and elsewhere, cable TV broadcasting was much more slow to develop. Instead, there was a huge boom in the sale of video recorders. Roughly half of British homes had a video by 1985 – a bigger percentage than in the United States – and the numbers kept on rising in the years that followed.

On both sides of the Atlantic the new technology changed viewing habits. People

Above Personal stereos became massively popular in the eighties. Headsets suited the health craze because they could be worn when taking exercise.

had much greater freedom to choose their evening's entertainment. And pop videos became a crucial part of teenage culture, whether made for MTV or home cassette players. Michael Jackson's *Thriller* (1983) was a landmark. It was produced like a mini-feature film and made by the respected director, Jon Landis, who had directed the brilliant spoof horror film, *An American Werewolf in London* (1981).

Hit films

One of the most influential youth films of the eighties was *Fame* (1980). It described the progress of a group of teenagers at New York City's High School for the Performing Arts. The scenes of high-energy dancing in the streets fired a new enthusiasm for modern dance, and the actors' costumes — leg warmers, leotards and jogging pants — influenced clothing styles. Above all, the idea of young people of different races and both sexes striving fiercely for success helped to set the mood of the time. *Fame* inspired a TV series of the same name, and the theme song of the film was a huge hit for vocalist Irene Cara.

Teenagers made up a vital section of the cinema-going audience in the United States and a wealth of films were made especially for the youth market. One star who specialized in teenage roles was Michael J.

Below The cinema decade opened with a burst of enthusiasm as the cast of *Fame* (1980) danced in the streets. Songs included *Red Light, I Sing the Body Electric* and *Fame (I'm Gonna Live Forever)*.

Fox. He appeared, for example, in *Back to the Future* (1985) and *Teen Wolf* (1985). Both films mixed realistic American backgrounds with elements of science fiction and horror.

The great fantasy film of the eighties, however, was *ET, the Extra-Terrestrial* (1982) about a lovable space alien who is befriended by a small boy in a suburb of Los Angeles. Directed by Steven Spielberg, the movie broke all box office records to become one of the biggest moneymakers of all time. A line spoken by the alien – 'ET go home' – also became one of the catch-phrases of the decade.

The conservative spirit of America in the eighties was reflected in the success of the series of Rambo movies, beginning with *First Blood* (1982), in which Sylvester Stallone played a Vietnam War veteran. The amount of violence worried many critics who also objected to the revival of 'macho' heroes – strong, hard men good at fighting but not particularly clever. Another macho figure, though more humorously treated, was the hero of *Crocodile Dundee* (1987). The film starred Paul Hogan as a manly but simple-minded Australian at large in New York City.

TV viewing

On TV, serials known as soaps triumphed over all other forms of entertainment. *Dallas*, about an oil-rich Texan family, won gigantic audiences all around the world. In the United States alone, a record 80 million people watched one episode in November 1980, to find out who shot the villain J. R. Ewing (played by actor Larry Hagman). *Dynasty*, another hugely successful soap, had an equally notorious villainess in Alexis, played by Joan Collins. Britain produced its own successful new soap in *EastEnders*, about life in a working-class community in the East End of London, and Australian soaps such as *Neighbours* also won surprise success on British TV. Teenage interest in these programmes was high, and Kylie Minogue, a star of *Neighbours*, went on to make several hit records.

Black actors made big breakthroughs on TV through programmes such as *The Cosby Show*, a situation comedy which

Below Actors Don Johnson (left) and Philip Michael Thomas (right) won world fame as the heroes of the stylish TV series *Miami Vice*.

Above The cast of *Dallas* celebrate the 250th episode of this hugely successful soap opera. The villain, J. R. Ewing, was played by Larry Hagman Jnr, seen in a blue shirt in the centre of the picture.

demonstrated that the tensions and the humour in black family life were much like those within white families. One of the most popular TV thriller series, *Miami Vice*, featured one black and one white detective. In this series great care was lavished on the heroes' designer clothes, the theme music was played on an electronic synthesizer and hit music often appeared as background tracks. *Miami Vice* was very much a show of the eighties.

Leisure

Cocktail bars and exclusive clubs became fashionable among older teenagers and young adults, although very few average teenagers ever entered the most expensive of the clubs. However, many ordinary discotheques deliberately cultivated a sophisticated image and became more selective about who they would admit.

Dance crazes of the time included break-dancing. This style developed among young black Americans, who might perform gymnastic feats such as back flips and head spins in mid-dance. 'Body popping' was similar, but involved making jerky, robotic gestures. Both break-dancing and body popping might be performed in the street or in shopping malls as a form of busking.

Above Break-dancers performed in plazas and shopping arcades. The craze was promoted as an alternative to violence and drugs.

A more short-lived craze was for so-called 'slam dancing'. Teenagers in combat boots, Levis and T-shirts simply slammed and piled into one another at dance halls. Although it received a lot of coverage in the media it probably involved little more than a desire to let off steam. The fad lasted only for a brief period around 1983.

Keeping fit

The great leisure trend was towards physical fitness. Perfecting the body was one of the ideals of the eighties and it took many forms. People jogged, or cycled, or went on marathon runs, for example. Aerobics became a household word; it referred to a system of physical exercises designed to speed up the breathing and stimulate blood circulation. Eurythmics was another term (from which the famous pop group took its name); it meant interpreting music through graceful body movements. America's best-selling video cassette in the mid-eighties was film star Jane Fonda's *Workout*.

Besides taking up physical exercise, teenagers were encouraged to avoid fatty foods, smoking and harmful food additives. The planet's own health raised concern, and the Green movement won widespread support among teenagers, aiming to defend the earth's natural resources against thoughtless exploitation by people.

Passing fads

In 1980–81 a baffling new craze swept the world. This was Rubik's Cube, a small cube puzzle invented by Hungarian Erno Rubik. It could be manipulated in many millions of different ways before a solution was found, and many people became obsessive about it. In fact, reasonably simple methods for solving the puzzle could be mastered with some practice. Techniques were learnt in school break times and teenagers often found themselves more skilled with a cube than their parents.

Around the same time a board game called Dungeons and Dragons was all the rage. It had a medieval fantasy setting, special dice and extraordinarily complicated rules. Again, teenagers developed skills that their parents could not hope to match.

Below Rubik's cube was a world-wide craze in the early eighties. Erno Rubik, the Hungarian inventor, became a millionaire.

In Britain, one of the most popular books of the eighties was *The Secret Diary of Adrian Mole, Aged 13¾*, humorously describing the life of a very average teenage boy. But few books could compete for excitement with the new video games. Space Invaders and other space theme games had arrived in the late seventies. The new range in the eighties was more varied and included Pac-Man, a pie-shaped creature who had to be guided through a maze while eating up dots on the screen. The craze for Pac-Man was such that teenagers could buy Pac-Man pens, Pac-Man pyjamas, Pac-Man hats and Pac-Man towels. Frogger, Donkey-Kong and Zaxxon were other new games. They might be played either on home computers, or in the new video arcades which opened up in the United States, Europe and elsewhere, often taking over from old pinball arcades. Many teenagers found intense thrills among their electronic blip-blips, their explosions and their flashing lights. Parents and other adults often worried that the young were developing a real addiction to the games, but that did not limit their appeal.

Problems of youth culture

Much more serious problems of addiction came from drug abuse. Drug-taking was a very alarming trend, especially among the young unemployed in big cities. In the United States, major government campaigns were launched to try and combat the spread of 'crack' (a form of cocaine), and everywhere heroin had become a menace. This highly addictive drug was much more dangerous than earlier generations of drugs used by some teenagers. Unlike marijuana, for example, heroin could kill through overdose. And it was also associated with a new medical peril, Aids.

Aids (Auto Immune Deficiency Syndrome) is a killer virus which was unheard of before the eighties. It spreads by attacking the body's immune system — its ability to resist disease. One of the ways in which it spreads is through the needles sometimes shared by heroin users. Addicts quickly became one of the groups of people most at risk.

Aids can also be transmitted from one person to another through sexual intercourse. Doctors advised young people against having sex with several partners, which obviously multiplied risks. More important still, they advised male teenagers to use condoms. These are rubber sheaths normally used to prevent pregnancy, which also offer vital protection against Aids.

The publicity given about Aids made many teenagers more cautious about sex

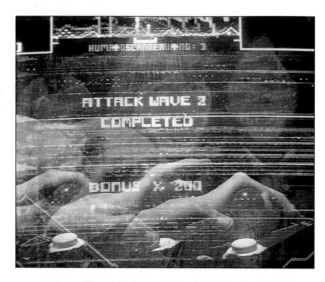

Above The video game craze, 1981. The fascinated faces of the players can be seen reflected in the screen of this electronic game.

Below Teenagers reading a government pamphlet about Aids. 'Don't die of ignorance' is the message. Before the eighties Aids was completely unknown.

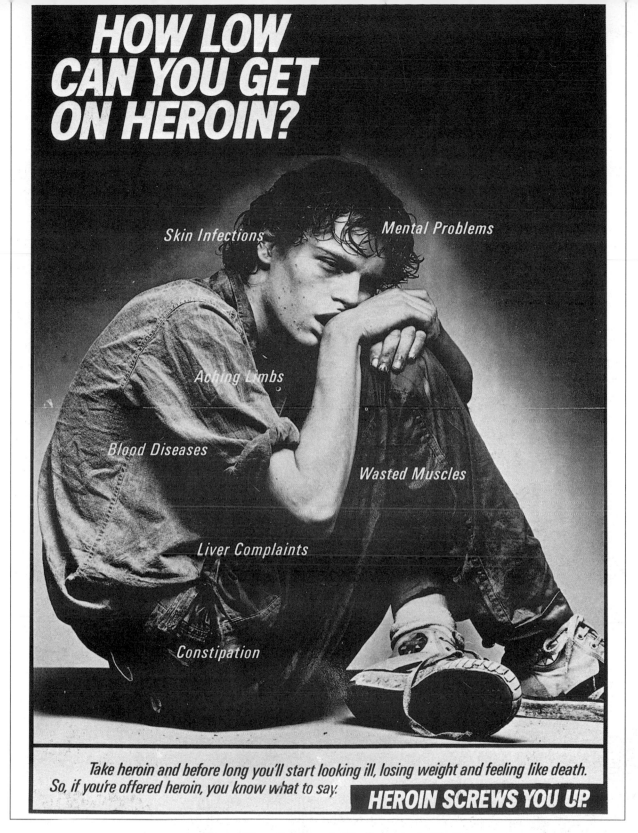

Above This poster was part of the Department of Health and Social Security's campaign to warn against the dangers of the highly addictive drug heroin.

Below A Christian congregation at prayer in the United States. These are charismatics who believe in direct personal experience of the Holy Spirit.

than earlier generations had been. And it may have helped to create a trend back towards the idea of choosing a single partner for life. Certainly, there was a strong reaction against permissiveness. In the United States there was a big revival of traditional moral values among Born Again Christians. These are people who have undergone an intense personal conversion to Christianity, often including the feeling of being reborn.

Born Again Christianity was less influential in other countries, but Christians and others did continue to challenge permissive values. Permissiveness was threatened especially in Muslim countries which were undergoing a big revival of faith. In 1989 Iran's Ayatollah Khomeini ordered that the British author Salman Rushdie be killed for writing a novel, *The Satanic Verses*. Devout Muslims throughout the world believed the book to be a blasphemy against Islam, though many disputed the Ayatollah's right to order a foreign author's death without trial.

Youth Cultures

In every decade since the Second World War, groups of teenagers have tended to form individual cultures, rather like tribes. Their clothing and musical tastes set them apart from adult society, but also from other youth cultures. There were mods and rockers in the sixties, for example, and punks and Rastafarians in the seventies. In the eighties, an extraordinary number of such tribes existed side by side. Many of them were nostalgic revivals from the past.

Above The psychedelic style, as revived in 1986. Few teenagers adopted the whole effect, but features such as floral shirts were popular.

Above A wild black bouffon hair-style, dark lipstick and heavy eye make-up all contribute to the look of the female Goth shown here.

New Romantics

The New Romantics wore very theatrical fashions. Some of the styles are described on page 6. The look was worn by both sexes, but the most exaggerated costumes were far too extreme to be seen much on the streets. New Romantics generally wore their finery in exclusive clubs.

Goths

Goths or Gothics were a new culture which emerged around the mid-eighties. Their style centred on all-black clothing, hair dyed jet black and sometimes black lipstick, all designed to emphasize pale white faces. Crucifixes might be worn too. The whole effect recalled the doom-laden zombies and vampires of horror films. Favourite groups included the Mission and the Cult.

Below The flat top might be dyed for extra effect. It was often worn with American clothing such as the baseball jacket seen here.

It is noticeable that male teenagers tend to set the style. Obviously, this is not because female teenagers are less fashion conscious, or less keen on music; it probably reflects the fact that young men are much more prone to form gangs.

Flat tops

People who wore the distinctive flat top haircut of the eighties were often clubland types. They tended to wear very fashionable clothing, usually American in style. Black jerseys were popular, too, and their favourite music often had a cool, jazzy sound associated with nightclubs and cocktail bars. The cover of Grace Jones's *Nightclubbing* album perfectly captures the look.

B-boys

Fans of hip hop and rap developed a casual style of their own. It centred around tracksuits, trainers and other items of sportswear, often worn with heavy gold rings and medallions. A ghetto blaster was part of the look.

Teddy boys and rockabillies

A number of eighties youth cultures recalled those of earlier decades. The Teddy boy style developed in Britain in the fifties, chiefly among working-class teenagers. The men wore Edwardian-style drape jackets, bootlace ties and quiff hair-styles, and women wore very full skirts. Rockabilly style also dated from the fifties and was built around denim jeans and jackets worn with cowboy shirts. The American confederate flag was a rockabilly emblem. The favourite music of both groups was rock'n'roll, and the rockabillies enjoyed country-and-western music too.

Mods and rudies

The original mods dated back to the sixties and created their style around sharp Italian suits, neatly styled hair, parkas and motor scooters. Mod girls wore pencil skirts and pale lipstick with a lot of eyeshadow. The rudie look was based on the two-tone suits and pork-pie hats worn by Britain's first generation Afro-Caribbeans. Both mods and rudies enjoyed Jamaican ska music, and groups such as Madness and the Specials won huge success in Britain in the early eighties by combining mod and rudie styles.

Below B-boy style was very informal and combined the two eighties crazes for rap music and sportswear. The ghetto blaster was an essential feature.

Skinheads

The original look emerged among British teenagers around 1969. Male skinheads wore closely cropped hair, Fred Perry shirts, braces and 'Doc Marten' boots. Female skinheads wore the same type of clothes. The style was built around the idea of looking 'hard' or aggressive. By the eighties skinheads had become closely associated with right wing views and racist violence.

Punks

Punks emerged around 1976 wearing clothing deliberately designed to shock: for example, ripped leathers with studs, chains, zips and safety pins as fashion accessories. Weird hairstyles were created, sometimes in day-glo colours, dyed with leopardskin patterning or shaped in a Mohican cut. Favourite punk groups included the Sex Pistols and the Clash.

Below Punk styles continued into the eighties, when some punks adopted the all-black 'Goth' look. This girl was photographed in Covent Garden, London.

Heavy metallers

This style was associated with motorbike gangs and had been around since the late sixties. Most heavy metallers were male, long haired and clad in leather or denim. Swastikas and death's head emblems were worn for shock effect. Heavy metal music was played by very loud drum-and-guitar groups including Slayer, Metallica, Judas Priest and Iron Maiden.

Psychedelics

Anyone wearing the swirling op art, paisley or psychedelic patterns of the sixties might come into this category. The term psychedelic means 'mind expanding' and it originally referred to drugs such as LSD which distort perception of reality, sometimes creating hallucinations. The Bangles were one of the groups of the eighties whose jangling guitars recalled the sixties sound.

Facing page Heavy metal fans. Their outfits include denim jackets worn with leather, badges and studs. One fan is playing an 'air guitar' — an imaginary guitar.

Eighties Style

People became very conscious of design in the eighties, and such terms as designer label and designer stubble reflected this new awareness.

In the early eighties the trend was very much for the 'hi-tech' or high-technology look. The idea was to celebrate the appearance of industrial buildings – oil refineries, warehouses and factories – with their metal piping and girders. Things should look 'functional', that is, be designed to reveal their practical purpose, with no frills or decoration. In the home, a shelving system might be made of plain metal racks, for example, instead of polished wood. Every new item, such as a Walkman stereo or a pocket camera was designed to look like a functional little 'black box' or 'steel box'.

Above This stereo headset is post-modernist in design. Unlike earlier 'black boxes' it is made of bright yellow plastic with trim in other colours.

Above The corner of this teenager's bedroom is in hi-tech style with its plain white walls and modern tubular shelving system.

system for filing information about work, home or social life. The Filofax was carried particularly by 'yuppies' – another catchword of the eighties. Yuppy stands for young urban professional and the word was often used to describe a certain type of ambitious young adult. Yuppies were often very hard working, but they were also keen to enjoy the pleasures of modern society such as designer clothes and CD players.

More generally, anything suggesting sophisticated new technology might be termed hi-tech. Examples included watches with the new digital face instead of old-fashioned hands on the dial; and the flat-screen TV introduced by Sony in 1982.

One personal item became a cult object. This was the Filofax, a portable ring binder

Computer design, synthetic materials

Ever since microchips first appeared in the seventies, computer technology had been transforming everyday life. Microchips are tiny wafers of silicon smaller than a postage stamp, which can serve as the main

Below A variety of digital watches became available in the eighties. One example shown here includes a miniature radio receiver, with headphones.

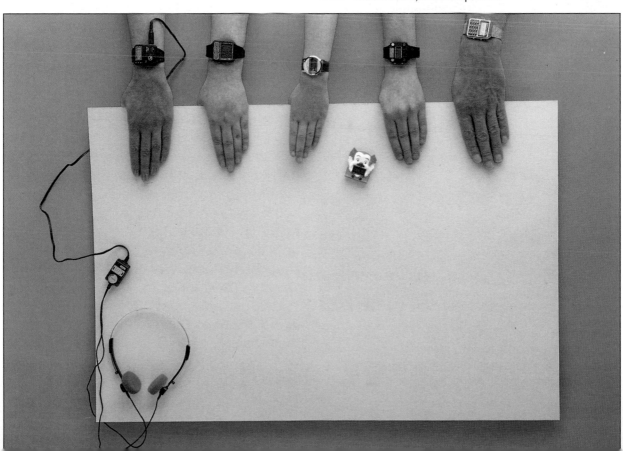

processing unit of a computer. They allowed a whole new generation of computers to be built, much smaller than earlier examples, so that they fitted on to a desk top at home, at school or in the office.

Designers in the eighties also used computers to perform very complex tasks, such as drawing 'three-dimensional' images on a screen. The body of a car, a spacecraft or a building, for example, would appear as a 'wireframe' image which could then be revolved and viewed from all angles. Computers offered a wealth of other possibilities. For example, TV's Max Headroom was a brilliant creation very popular among older teenagers. He was the comic host of a TV video show, and was played by an actor in latex make-up. To make

Max look like a half-human robot, images of him were mixed under computer control with background graphics which were also generated by computer. The effects were weirdly disconcerting — and hilarious.

Designers in the eighties were keen to use new synthetic materials. One of the most remarkable creations of the time was the C5, an electric tricycle launched by Clive Sinclair (the chief pioneer of home computers). The vehicle's body shell was made entirely of moulded polypropylene, a type of plastic, and the C5 was steered by handlebars beneath the rider's knees. The idea was to try and replace petrol-driven cars for short journeys in cities. Sadly, however, the C5 failed to catch on, partly because the light, synthetic body offered so little protection amid city traffic. Shortly after the launch in 1985, production was halted.

Above Computer graphics allowed designers to create complex images on the computer screen, and then bend them or revolve them through three dimensions.

Post-modernism

The original hi-tech look stressed strict, functional simplicity in design. But during the eighties another trend emerged and caught on strongly with the public. This has been called the 'post-modernist' movement and it encouraged little decorative flourishes in design, with licks of colour and a sense of fun.

One famous example in architecture was the Public Services Building at Portland, Oregon, in the United States. Completed in 1983, it was designed by American architect Michael Graves in a colourful style reminiscent of ancient Egyptian furnishing. Another influence was the Memphis group of furniture designers in Italy. At the Milan Furniture Fair of 1981, they produced a lot of items in bright, jazzy colours with patterns that recalled fabrics such as leopardskin which were much used in the fifties. Ideas like these had long been thought bad taste, but

Above The Public Services Building at Portland in Oregon is an example of post-modernist architecture. Coloured decoration and features such as these triangular blocks help to give interest and variety to its appearance.

the trend continued. Another Italian designer, Michele de Lucchi, came up with designs for everyday items such as vacuum cleaners and toasters that made them look like children's toys.

Colour and fun entered high street stores as designers started to challenge the functional 'black box' look. Torches, watches, cameras and personal stereos were now produced in coloured plastic as 'fashion accessories'. Typical colours included lilac, flamingo pink, bright yellow and a slightly acid green. Teenagers could buy goods to match the colours of their favourite fashion outfit, so that they had a design look from head to toe.

Images of the Eighties

Royal wedding

On 29 July 1981 Prince Charles, heir to the British throne, married Lady Diana Spencer, the shy, attractive daughter of one of Britain's well-to-do families. The wedding took place in St Paul's Cathedral in London and 700 million TV viewers all around the world watched as the couple walked down the aisle. The young bride was wearing a billowing wedding dress of ivory silk, with an immensely long train. It gave her the look of 'a fairytale princess' and contributed to the fashionable New Romantic look of the early eighties. Afterwards the couple rode to Buckingham Palace in a horse-drawn carriage. They kissed on the palace balcony before a vast, cheering crowd.

Above The Prince and Princess of Wales on the balcony at Buckingham Palace, July 1981.

Afghanistan

Afghanistan is a mountainous land which borders the Soviet Union. In December 1979 the Russians invaded the country to support a pro-Soviet government which seemed on the edge of collapse. Civil war erupted. The Afghan government and its Soviet allies controlled the towns, while resistance fighters waged a fierce guerilla war from the hills. The main resistance group was the Muslim Mujahedin, whose members believed that they were fighting a jihad or holy war against the enemy.

The war dragged on through the eighties. The 115,000 Russian troops found themselves hampered by poor roads and rocky terrain, and they could not defeat the guerillas. The war had also created a serious rift between the Soviet Union and the United States. Eventually, Soviet leader Mikhail Gorbachev ordered a Russian withdrawal. The last Soviet troops left Afghanistan in February 1989.

Above An Afghan rebel photographed in 1981. Such tribesmen used guerilla tactics to harrass the Soviet invaders until their withdrawal in 1989.

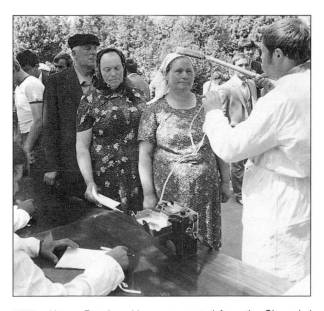

Above Russian citizens evacuated from the Chernobyl area are checked for radiation levels after the nuclear accident in the spring of 1986.

Disaster at Chernobyl

In April 1986 an accident struck one of the Soviet Union's nuclear power stations. The plant was at Chernobyl, about 130 km north of the city of Kiev. One of the reactors there was badly damaged and a seemingly uncontrollable fire raged in its core. Clouds of radioactive material leaked into the atmosphere and were carried by winds over places as far distant as Norway, Sweden, Finland and Britain. The Soviet Union had to evacuate the entire area around the plant itself, and needed expert help from other countries to control the fire. Although only two people were reported killed it was certain that more would eventually die from radiation poisoning. Many people began to question the safety of nuclear power.

Space shuttle

America's space shuttle made its maiden flight on 12 April 1981. The importance of the craft was the winged orbiter, about the size of an airliner. Launched by booster rockets, the orbiter was designed to carry payloads such as satellites into orbit, then glide back to Earth to be used again.

Many successful flights were made, and among the crews was Sally Ride, America's first woman in space. In January 1986, however, disaster struck. Only a few seconds after the twenty-fifth shuttle mission was launched a horrific explosion destroyed the spacecraft. All seven people on board died instantly. They included a high school teacher who had been chosen as the first private citizen to fly in a shuttle. Shuttle flights began again in 1988, by which time the Soviet Union was setting new records for space endurance.

Lebanon

Lebanon was one of the world's most troubled regions. The country lies at the eastern end of the Mediterranean, bordering Israel to the south. As a result of Arab-Israeli fighting a large number of Palestinian refugees and guerillas entered the country during the seventies. Lebanon has its own rich mix of peoples, including three main sects of Muslims and a strong Christian element. The new arrivals contributed to mounting rivalries which erupted in almost permanent civil war.

By 1980, 33 private armies or militias were fighting for control. Syria invaded the country to try and help the Muslims; the Israelis invaded to try and drive out Palestinian guerillas. A United Nations peace-keeping force tried but failed to keep order. Nothing seemed capable of ending the strife. Gunfire, bombings, kidnappings and assassinations continued throughout the eighties.

One technique of the militias was to seize foreign hostages, often Americans or Europeans. Terry Waite, a special representative of the Archbishop of Canterbury, was skilled at negotiating the release of such hostages, but in 1987 he was himself kidnapped and held hostage.

War in the Falklands

The bleak little island group of the Falklands lies about 800 km from the mainland of South America. It has been a British colony since 1833, and the inhabitants are mostly of British descent. However, Argentina has long laid claim to the islands, and prospects of valuable oil deposits offshore made the dispute worse. In April 1982 the Argentines made a surprise attack on the Falklands and put them under military occupation. In reply, Mrs Thatcher sent a British force to win them back. A short, bloody war followed in which over a thousand British and Argentinian

servicemen lost their lives. The result was a British victory, and afterwards Britain continued to keep a garrison of some 4,000 troops on the islands.

Above The Argentinian cruiser *General Belgrano* is sunk by a British ship in May 1982, during the first major encounter of the Falklands War.

Below Damage from Israeli bombings in West Beirut, 1982. The Israelis mounted a full-scale invasion in that year and did not leave until 1985.

Above Victims of drought in Ethiopia. Thousands of starving refugees took shelter in relief camps, and TV pictures of them stirred consciences world-wide.

Famine in Ethiopia

Terrible famine plagued Ethiopia in the eighties. This country of poor herdsmen and farmers experienced its longest-running drought of recent times. The government was also involved in a long civil war and devoted much of its energy to the fighting. The result was hunger on a horrific scale. By mid-1985 more than 250,000 people had died of starvation. Thousands of refugees took shelter at famine relief camps and pictures of their suffering were seen on TV screens all around the world. In response, a massive international relief operation was mounted. The famine also stirred the consciences of pop stars who gave their services free to make the charity record *Do They Know It's Christmas?* and took part in the Live Aid concert.

Iranian Embassy siege

Iran was ruled from 1979 to 1989 by the Islamic religious leader the Ayatollah Khomeini. The country was at war with its neighbour Iraq throughout much of the eighties. It was also bitterly hostile to the United States, and the focus of many tensions elsewhere in the world.

In May 1980, for example, gunmen hostile to the Ayatollah took over the Iranian Embassy in Knightsbridge, London. They demanded the release of political prisoners held in Iran and started to kill hostages to show that they meant business. In reply, Britain's anti-terrorist SAS (Special Air Service) made a spectacular assault on the building. TV cameras followed as black-clad figures wearing balaclavas burst into the embassy armed with smoke grenades and sub-machine guns. Four out of the five gunmen were killed and all the surviving nineteen hostages were brought to safety.

Solidarity in Poland

Food shortages and other problems led to widespread unrest in Poland. In 1980 there was a wave of workers' strikes which gave birth to the Solidarity movement. This was the first independent trade union in Eastern Europe and it threatened vast changes in Polish society. For 16 months Solidarity flourished. Then the country's new leader, General Jaruzelski, acted firmly against the union. He declared martial law, ordered mass arrests and banned Solidarity. The situation had eased by the end of 1983 but workers and government remained suspicious of one another. Lech Walesa, leader of Solidarity, was given the Nobel Peace Prize for 1983, in tribute to his union's stand. By the end of the decade, the Polish government was showing signs of greater tolerance towards Solidarity, and of allowing them to play a greater part in the political process.

Above Helped by an SAS man, a hostage climbs to safety at the climax of the Iranian Embassy seige in Knightsbridge, London, in May 1980.

Below Slogans and striking workers at the Lenin shipyard in Gdansk, Poland, photographed in 1980. Gdansk was a centre of the Solidarity movement.

Reagan and Thatcher

The two figures who dominated politics in the United States and Britain were President Ronald Reagan and Prime Minister Margaret Thatcher. Both pursued conservative policies at home. Both were also firmly anti-communist, and they increased spending on defence. In 1983 President Reagan sent US marines into the Caribbean island of Grenada to stop a communist takeover, and he also urged American support for *Contra* guerillas fighting the left-wing government of Nicaragua in Central America.

President Reagan and Prime Minister Thatcher were both plagued by a severe recession, or slump in world trade, during the early years of the eighties. Unemployment in the United States and Britain was then very high. By the mid-eighties, however, there were signs of economic recovery.

Below President Reagan and Prime Minister Thatcher inspect a model of the space shuttle. The two leaders developed a strong friendship for one another.

Gorbachev

In March 1985 a new leader came to power in the Soviet Union. His name was Mikhail Gorbachev and, aged 54, he was much younger than his predecessors. He was also keen to reform the Soviet system which, he believed, had failed to keep pace with developments in the modern world. Gorbachev called for greater democracy: voters should be given a proper choice of candidates in elections. He called for a new spirit of *glasnost*, or openness, in public life. And he also called for *perestroika*, or reconstruction, in society as a whole. Gorbachev travelled widely abroad and his reforming spirit helped to ease tensions between East and West. In December 1987 he and President Reagan signed a major new arms control agreement. This treaty covered Intermediate Range Nuclear Forces (INF); that is, nuclear weapons of medium range. It was enormously important in reducing fears of a nuclear war.

Above Soviet leader Mikhail Gorbachev talks to workers at a car factory in Moscow. He was keen to reform Soviet industry and increase output.

The Green Movement

Pressure groups, like Greenpeace and Friends of the Earth, were active in many parts of the world during the eighties. Through daring protests they raised green issues and helped to put care of the environment high on the political agenda. Many governments are now keen to show that they are actively promoting policies which help to conserve rainforests, protect the atmosphere, combat acid rain, and preserve wildlife in danger of extinction. It is yet to be seen how effective these policies will prove to be.

Left Members of Greenpeace – the environmental pressure group – protest against the pollution of the seas and oceans by the dumping of chemical and nuclear waste.

Glossary

Aerobics A system of physical exercise aiming to speed up breathing and get the blood circulating.

Aids (Auto Immune Deficiency Syndrome) A lethal virus disease which spread rapidly throughout the world in the mid-eighties. It can be transmitted by sexual intercourse, or through the mingling of one person's blood with another (as may happen when heroin addicts share a needle, for example).

CND (Campaign for Nuclear Disarmament) A movement founded in Britain in 1958 to press for the abolition of nuclear weapons. CND gained many new recruits in the early eighties as fear of nuclear war grew. Campaigners wanted unilateral or one-sided disarmament; that is, they believed that Britain should give up its nuclear weapons whether other countries did or not.

Cable TV A television system in which programmes are sent to receivers by cable. It is only for subscribers; that is, people who pay for the system.

Cocaine A very strong, addictive stimulant drug derived from the South American coca plant. It usually appears in the form of a white powder. In the eighties an even more dangerous new form of cocaine appeared – 'crack'. It spread especially among unemployed teenagers in the United States. Deaths sometimes occurred among users, who were also prone to intense depression when off the drug.

Communism A political theory aiming to establish a society where major enterprises such as factories, mines, farms and shops are owned by all citizens rather than a class of wealthy people. In practice, Communist societies have tended to create powerful state authorities which control those enterprises.

Condom A thin rubber sheath designed to cover the penis during sexual intercourse.

Conservative A word to describe people who wish to hold on to established customs and values. People described as conservative are generally cautious of any change, unless the change is a return to earlier practices.

Contras Right-wing guerillas in Nicaragua, campaigning to overthrow the elected government.

Contraceptive Any device used to prevent an unwanted pregnancy.

Designer label A label visible on clothing which proves that it comes from a prominent fashion house.

Feminism The movement aiming to win full rights and respect for women in society, and to celebrate the special qualities of the female sex. At a US airbase at Greenham Common in Britain, an all-women peace camp was formed to protest against nuclear weapons. In 1982, 30,000 women from Britain, Europe and the United States joined hands to 'embrace the base', leaving tokens such as baby clothes on the fence.

Glasnost A policy of openness introduced by Mikhail Gorbachev in the Soviet Union. It permitted greater freedom of discussion in the media, for example.

Green movement The movement to protect the earth's natural resoures against, for example, pollution of the seas and atmosphere, or destruction of forests and animal species.

Heroin A dangerous and highly addictive drug derived from morphine. It is basically narcotic; that is, it slows down the body system. An overdose can result in death.

Hi tech   The high-technology design style of the early eighties. It was originally based on the functional look of industrial buildings, but might include anything which suggested advanced modern technology.

Homosexual (or **gay**)   Someone who is attracted to members of the same sex.

Laser   A device using the energy of intensely pure light. The first lasers appeared in the sixties, and by the eighties they were performing a host of tasks from eye surgery to use in compact disc players.

Microchip   A tiny chip of silicon containing the circuits for a computer.

MTV (Music Television)   The rock music video channel on American cable TV.

Perestroika   The policy introduced by Mikhail Gorbachev to try and reform and rebuild society in the Soviet Union. *Perestroika* is a Russian word meaning 'reconstruction'.

Radioactivity   The emission of waves or particles after a nuclear reaction occurs. A nuclear explosion or the leakage of material from a nuclear plant can cause radiation sickness. Symptoms range from headache and nausea to cancer and death.

Recession   A slowing down in business activity.

Unemployment   The condition of being out of work. Unemployment was at its worst in the mid-eighties when there were over 11 million out of work in the United States and some 3 million in Britain.

Further Reading

At the time of writing very little has been published on the eighties as a decade. However, the following books provide useful background reading:

Chronicle of the 20th Century (Longman, 1988)

The World Almanac and Book of Facts (New Enterprises Association, 1988)

You'll Never Be 16 Again, Peter Everett (BBC Publications, 1986)

British Hit Singles, Paul Gambaccini, Tim Rice and Jo Rice (Guinness Superlatives Ltd, 1987)

Design Source Book, Penny Sparke and others (Macdonald, 1986)

Additionally, the following offer a humorous view of a British teenager's life in the early eighties:

The Secret Diary of Adrian Mole, Aged 13¾, Sue Townsend (Methuen, 1982)

The Growing Pains of Adrian Mole, Sue Townsend (Methuen, 1984)

Picture Acknowledgements

Architectural Association 37; Barnaby's Picture Library 35t; Daily Telegraph Colour Library (Andrew McKim) 36; DHSS 27; Greenpeace/Walker 45b; Lesley Howling *front cover*; Hutchison Library 6, 32; Kobal Collection 20, 21; Photri 7, 19, 25, 28, 38, 40, 43b, 44, 45t; Redferns 13, 14, 15; Rex Features 10b, 16, 33; TOPHAM 4, 5, 8, 9, 11, 12, 17t, 17b, 18, 22l, 22r, 23, 24, 26t, 26b, 29, 31, 34, 35b, 39t, 39b, 41t, 41b, 42, 43t; Wayland 10t, 30t, 30b.

Index